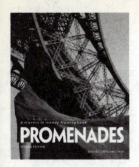

Lab Manual

MITCHELL | MITSCHKE | TANO

VISTA®
HIGHER LEARNING

Boston, Massachusetts

Photography and Art Credits
All images © Vista Higher Learning unless otherwise noted.

Cover José Blanco; **19** Martín Bernetti; **21** (tl) Ventus Pictures; (tm, tr, bl, br) Martín Bernetti.

ISBN: 978-1-61857-018-5

5 6 7 8 9 BB 18 17 16

Printed in the United States of America.